I AM FOR YOU

I AM FOR YOU

MIEKO OUCHI

Playwrights Canada Press
Toronto

For professional or amateur production rights, please contact:
Ian Arnold at Catalyst TCM
#312 - 100 Broadview Avenue, Toronto, ON M4M 3H3
416.645.0935, ian@catalysttmc.com

LIBRARY AND ARCHIVES CANADA CATALOGUING IN PUBLICATION

Ouchi, Mieko, author
        I am for you / by Mieko Ouchi.

A play.
Issued in print and electronic formats.
ISBN 978-1-77091-511-4 (paperback).--ISBN 978-1-77091-512-1 (pdf).--
ISBN 978-1-77091-514-5 (mobi).--ISBN 978-1-77091-513-8 (epub)

        I. Title.

PS8579.U26I12 2016   C812'.6   C2016-905701-1
                                         C2016-905702-X

We acknowledge the financial support of the Canada Council for the Arts, the Ontario Arts Council (OAC), the Ontario Media Development Corporation, and the Government of Canada through the Canada Book Fund for our publishing activities. Nous remercions l'appui financier du Conseil des Arts du Canada, le Conseil arts de l'Ontario (CAO), la Société de développement de l'industrie des médias de l'Ontario, et le Gouvernement du Canada par l'entremise du Fonds du livre du Canada pour nos activités d'édition.

MERCUTIO
Tybalt, you rat-catcher, will you walk?

TYBALT
What wouldst thou have with me?

MERCUTIO
Good king of cats, nothing but one of your nine
lives; that I mean to make bold withal, and as you
shall use me hereafter, drybeat the rest of the
eight. Will you pluck your sword out of his pitcher
by the ears? Make haste, lest mine be about your
ears ere it be out.

TYBALT
I am for you.

They fight.

I Am For You was premiered by Concrete Theatre (Edmonton, Alberta) on November 12, 2013, with the following cast and crew:

Lainie   Samantha Jeffery
Mariam   Patricia Cerra
Caddell Morris   Jonathan Purvis

Directed by Mieko Ouchi
Set, Props, and Lighting Design by Patrick Beagan
Costume Design by Mieko Ouchi
Sound Design by Dave Clarke
Stage Managed by Rachel Rudd
Touring Technical Support by Josiah Hiemstra

The playwright acknowledges the assistance of the 2013 Banff Playwrights Colony—a partnership between The Banff Centre and the Canada Council for the Arts.

The playwright also acknowledges the support of the Enbridge playRites Award for an Established Canadian Playwright and the NotaBle Acts Theatre Festival.

CHARACTERS

Lainie	seventeen, a fighter
Mariam	seventeen, a fencer
Caddell Morris	twenty-seven, a student teacher,
	Voice of Benvolio,
	Voice of Lord Capulet

A high school drama room. The present.

Two girls appear. Opposite sides of the stage. They look out at the audience.

LAINIE   I don't know how it starts.

MARIAM   I don't know why it happens.

LAINIE   But sometimes I get this tiny feeling inside.

MARIAM   It's there. All the time. I feel it.

BOTH   Judgment.

LAINIE   I hate it when people make assumptions about me.

MARIAM   I *hate* it.

LAINIE   When that happens, that tiny feeling . . . it starts to build.

MARIAM   It grows and grows until I feel like I'm going to burst.

LAINIE   And all I can think is.

MARIAM   I know what they're thinking.

LAINIE	I can see it in their eyes.
MARIAM	But they don't know me.
LAINIE	They don't know me at all.
BOTH	And then all it takes . . .
LAINIE	. . . is a look.
MARIAM	. . . or a word.
LAINIE	. . . or a brush.
MARIAM	. . . or a push.
LAINIE	And it's on.
MARIAM	It's so on.

They fight. Vicious. Messy. Not a girl fight.

CADDELL appears. Instantly, the fight freezes.

Shift.

CADDELL   The funny thing is . . . I woke up this morning and thought to myself . . . this is the beginning. The first day of the next stage of my life. I won't lie, it's been a hard road getting here . . . but for the first time in a long time, I can honestly say . . . I feel . . . truly excited. Standing at the bottom of a mountain looking up, yeah, but ready . . . I think. I hope. I guess we'll see.

I have my first official coffee meeting with the drama teacher, Mrs. Lee. She seems excited to have someone with my theatre skills on board for a practicum. The timing's perfect. She needs help on their fall production of *Romeo and Juliet*. We talk plans for rehearsal. Unbelievable. Talk through some workshops I can lead with the cast and some of her classes. Amazing. Talk about her vision of the play. Fantastic . . .

Then she asks me for one small favour.

She asks if I can go supervise the Drama Club after school for a half-hour. They know what they're supposed to do. Just needs someone in the room to oversee until she gets there. I say no problem. Easy. I'm on top of it.

I mean, honestly, how hard can it be to supervise some kids painting some flats, you know, for the walls, for the play?

He arrives in the drama room. The girls are in full fight.

Stop. Stop. Stop it!

He pulls them apart. They are spitting mad, red-faced, furious.

What's going on here?

They go for each other again.

Hey! Hey!

He manages to separate them.

(to LAINIE) Don't even think about it.

(to MARIAM) Stay there.

They all turn. A group of other kids has just arrived.

Hey . . . everyone . . . come on in . . . I'm Caddell, Mr. Morris. Your new student teacher. Mrs. Lee asked me to get you started on the set. She's going to be a little late. So, do you want to go down to the storage room and start pulling out the flats? We've got some painting to do . . .

Everyone, including the girls, goes to leave.

Not you two.

They stop.

What just happened here?

Nothing.

I shouldn't even be standing here discussing this. I should be hauling both of you down to the principal. What is going on?

LAINIE is upset. She stops herself from saying something.

What?

LAINIE   *(fierce)* It doesn't matter.

CADDELL   Talk to me, or we're going.

Nothing. He looks at MARIAM, who looks away. She's no rat.

Fine. Let's go.

He starts for the door. LAINIE kicks the wall.

You have something you want to say?

Finally.

LAINIE   You take me down there, I'm gonna get kicked out.

CADDELL   Yeah, well maybe missing a class or two isn't such a bad idea. You both need some time to cool down.

LAINIE   Not class . . .

*MARIAM snickers. LAINIE's face turns red. She almost goes for
her again.*

CADDELL   *(to MARIAM)* Enough . . . *(to LAINIE)* What do you mean?

MARIAM   This is stupid. Let's just go—

LAINIE   —shut up—

MARIAM   —take us down there. It doesn't matter to me. I was
           defending myself. They're not going to kick *me* out of
           school.

LAINIE   Shut up, Mariam—

CADDELL   —hey!

MARIAM   You're new, so you don't know who Lainie is, but *this*
           happens all the time. This is how she is. She's always
           pushing / people around. Picking fights.

LAINIE   / screw you—

CADDELL   —hey! Enough.

MARIAM   You just picked me because you thought you I was an
           easy target. / You just thought you could make your-
           self look good because I wouldn't fight back—

LAINIE   / No, I didn't. I punched you because you think you're
           better than all of us and someone needs to tune you
           in—

CADDELL   I should be taking you down to the Office. Or at least
           hauling you down to Mrs. Lee.

MARIAM   That's so unfair! I didn't do anything.

LAINIE   Yes, you did! You shoved me first—

CADDELL   —enough!

LAINIE   Fine. You know what? Take us down to the principal and get it over with. I don't care about this stupid play. Or this freaking school. I'm done.

She heads for the door.

CADDELL   No, you're not.

LAINIE stops and turns back. CADDELL is thinking on his feet.

          What if we make a deal?

MARIAM   A deal?

LAINIE   *(realizing)* Ugh. I know what you're gonna do.

CADDELL   Hey . . . Lainie . . . right? You don't even know what I'm going to say.

LAINIE   Yes, I do. You're gonna make us do something like write a play about how bad it is to fight and make us do it in the cafeteria at lunch or something. So you can put it on your resumé. We're not idiots. We've had student teachers before.

CADDELL   Actually, that's not what I was thinking at all.

LAINIE   Right.

CADDELL   I just figured, you want to fight each other, right? So, let's do it.

MARIAM   What? Teachers can't get students to fight.

CADDELL   Sure they can.

LAINIE   What is this? Some sick *Hunger Games* type thing?[1]

CADDELL   Not at all. I was going to ask for some volunteers, but now I don't need to. Here's the deal. You show up Saturday at 10:00 a.m. Here. You spend the day with me.

LAINIE   A detention.

MARIAM   No . . . you're right. He *is* gonna make us talk about it. Just not in the cafeteria. How we could handle it differently. Stupid conflict resolution or whatever.

CADDELL   It's up to you. As deals go, it's pretty sweet. You show up. You do your time. Then we're cool.

The girls look at each other. Reluctantly look back at him. Fine.

Good.

They exit. He watches them go.

(to himself) First day . . .

Shift.

He turns out to us. He addresses Mrs. Lee.

Mrs. Lee?

Can I talk to you?

I . . . no, things went just fine. Pretty . . . smooth . . . it's just . . . um . . . well there was a bit of a disagreement happening in the room when I got there.

No, two *girls*, actually.

---

1   May be updated to something more current if desired.

No. Nothing much. I handled it. I'm just wondering. Would it be cool if I worked with them this weekend? Instead of pulling some kids from the club like we talked about? It'll be useful. And who knows, these two might benefit a little from working together . . .

Absolutely. It's good to know you're around. And I'll come straight down to the art room if there's any trouble. But they'll be fine. I'm sure of it.

He nods.

Okay.

He waves. She's gone. He exits.

Shift.

Saturday morning. Ten a.m. on the dot.

MARIAM arrives in the drama room. The school's theatre. She looks around.

MARIAM   Hello?

Hello?

Nothing. No one has shown.

What the—

She goes to leave.

LAINIE   —he's not here.

LAINIE appears. She has been waiting, sitting in the seats at the back of the theatre.

MARIAM   Great.

They size each other up. They're alone. LAINIE crosses down.

LAINIE Maybe he just wanted us to sort it out on our own.

MARIAM What's that supposed to mean?

LAINIE He said he wanted us to fight.

MARIAM I'm not afraid of you, Lainie.

    LAINIE just laughs. Oh really?

    I'm not. I think you're full of crap.

LAINIE Shut up.

MARIAM Jam-packed.

LAINIE You wanna come over here and say that?

MARIAM I'd be careful if I was you. You don't know me. You don't know anything about me.

LAINIE Yes, I do. You're all lippy and in my face when the teacher's around, let's see how you do on your own—

They're about to fight.

CADDELL —good morning.

CADDELL is in the door, a bag in his hand.

    Glad you both could make it.

LAINIE What's that?

He puts down the bag and pulls out a foil. He swipes it dramatically through the air.

CADDELL What does it look like?

11

LAINIE   We're gonna fight with swords?

CADDELL   Fencing foils, actually.

CADDELL tosses them each a fencing jacket. MARIAM starts putting it on. LAINIE too.

          They designed them as training weapons back in the 1700s so they could teach the art of swordplay without people actually killing each other.

LAINIE   So this is what you meant when you said we were gonna fight?

CADDELL   Yep.

MARIAM says nothing. She grabs a foil and does a quick salute.

MARIAM   En garde.

She hits En garde stance, ready to go.

LAINIE   *(shocked, turning on CADDELL)* You think this is my fault. You totally set this up so she can kick my—

CADDELL   *(equally surprised)* —actually I had no idea.

LAINIE   Yeah, right.

CADDELL   Interesting twist, though.

MARIAM   Scared?

LAINIE stares at her, her pride kicking in. How hard can it be? She grabs a foil.

LAINIE   This thing's light.

She quickly feels the blade to see if it's sharp. It's not. It's bendy.

CADDELL   No blade on a foil. It's a thrusting weapon.

She feels the end of it to see how sharp it is.

They're blunted. So no one gets hurt.

LAINIE gets into some kind of ready position that resembles a softball hitter's stance. No form. But she's ready for a battle.

LAINIE   Okay. Let's do this.

CADDELL   *(leaping in)* Whoa. Whoa. Whoa. That's not how we're rolling here. Safety first. Blunted or not, they're still weapons.

He tosses them both a mask.

These go on before *any* engagement with the foils. Clear?

LAINIE   Fine.

She puts it on. He looks at MARIAM.

CADDELL   *(mispronouncing her name)* Marian?

MARIAM   Yes!

She is still in En garde. Ready.

CADDELL   Marian, make this a *little* fairer. At least show her a grip.

LAINIE snickers.

MARIAM   *(furious)* My name's not Maria*n*. It's Maria*m*.

CADDELL   I'm sorry. Maria*m*? C'mon. Help her out.

MARIAM looks at him. Finally she drops her En garde. Pulls off her mask.

MARIAM   Here. *(She demonstrates angrily to LAINIE.)* Like this. *(to CADDELL)* I use a pistol grip.

Seeing LAINIE's confusion.

          That's what real fencers use. These are like . . . old-fashioned French handles.

CADDELL   Worked for Cyrano.

          De Bergerac?

Nothing. They are both deadly serious.

          Just saying.

MARIAM goes back to her side. Gets back into En garde.

MARIAM   I'm not used to fencing dry.

LAINIE   *(to CADDELL)* What's that supposed to mean?

CADDELL   That means Mariam fences competitively. She's used to using electronic targets and a charged foil.

LAINIE   *(turning on CADDELL)* This is totally unfair!

CADDELL   Well, to tell you the truth, I wasn't expecting either of you to have fenced. *(to LAINIE)* Is it okay if I put my hands on your shoulders? To adjust your position?

LAINIE   Yeah. I guess.

CADDELL takes her by the shoulders and positions her across from MARIAM. He turns her.

CADDELL   Sideways, you're a narrower target. All right, good.
           Let's learn some basics so you two can start fighting.

*This is getting real. LAINIE looks at him, starting to panic. Are
they really going to do this?*

LAINIE   This is crazy. Do you even know what you're doing?

CADDELL   Of course I do. I did a theatre degree before I went
           back to become a teacher.

LAINIE   . . . So you were like an actor or something?

CADDELL   Yeah . . . or something. I took stage fighting at the-
           atre school and I loved it. So I kept training while I
           worked as an actor. So . . . yes, I know how to do this.

MARIAM   *(realizing)* You're working on *Romeo and Juliet.*

CADDELL   Smart girl. For part of my practicum I'm choreo-
           graphing the fights for the show. And teaching a little
           stage combat to the whole cast.

           Two households, both alike in dignity,
           In fair Verona, where we lay our scene,
           From ancient grudge break to new mutiny,
           Where civil blood makes civil hands unclean.

The girls look at him blankly.

           The opening lines of the play? Didn't you read *Romeo
           and Juliet* in English class?

MARIAM pushes her mask up onto her forehead.

MARIAM   We did *Hamlet.*

CADDELL   Ooh. Poor you. Lainie?

She shrugs. She takes her mask off too.

15

LAINIE   I don't remember.

CADDELL   What do you think those lines mean?

MARIAM   *(looking at LAINIE)* They don't like each other?

CADDELL   More than that. They mean the two families fight. Right there in the street.

LAINIE   The play starts with a fight?

CADDELL   Yep. Right off the bat. Shakespeare knew his audience pretty well, hunh? Fights grab people's attention.

Also, when he wrote the play, people still carried swords. Fights were breaking out every day. It was actually a huge problem for the police at the time. So Shakespeare put that in the script.

It doesn't last long though. The Prince of Verona shows up and shuts the whole thing down. He says:

Stepping between them.

> *Rebellious subjects, enemies to peace,*
> *On pain of torture, from those bloody hands*
> *Throw your mistemper'd weapons to the ground.*

When they hear "on pain of torture," everyone stops fighting and drops their weapons.

LAINIE   Why?

CADDELL   Why did you two stop when I came in? Because he's the Prince and he has the power to get them into big trouble. He warns them . . .

> *Three civil brawls, bred of an airy word,*
> *By thee, old Capulet,*

He gestures to one girl. Then to the other.

> and Montague,
> *Have thrice disturb'd the quiet of our streets,*
> *If ever you disturb our streets again,*
> *Your lives shall pay the forfeit of the peace.*
>
> Basically he tells the two heads of the households,
> you do this again, you're dead . . . that's how the play
> starts.

MARIAM   How do you know all the lines?

CADDELL   I've done the play. Second year of university, and then
again in the park.

LAINIE   You played Romeo?

CADDELL   Actually I played Benvolio the first time. He's one of
Romeo's friends . . . And then yeah, actually I did get
to play Romeo.

MARIAM   I thought he was supposed to be young?

CADDELL turns and looks at her.

CADDELL   Take it easy. Teachers have feelings too, you know . . .

MARIAM   I *meant* . . . like isn't he supposed to be seventeen or
something. Like our age.

CADDELL   I thought you said you didn't read the play.

MARIAM   I saw the movie. In *class*. Everyone's seen the movie.

CADDELL   It doesn't actually say how old he is in the play, but
yeah, he's probably around seventeen or eighteen.
For the record . . . I wasn't *that* much older when I
played him.

LAINIE	*(sceptical)* Mn. Hm.
CADDELL	Anyway . . . here's the deal. Yes, I've done the show a few times as an actor, but I've never gotten to choreograph the fights. So . . .
MARIAM	*(realizing)* . . . that's why we're here. To be your guinea pigs.
CADDELL	*(smiles)* I figure if I can teach you . . .
MARIAM	*(quickly)* I'm up for it.
CADDELL	Lainie?

Now that she's seen MARIAM's skill, she's not so sure she wants to fight after all. But . . .

LAINIE	Fine.
CADDELL	All right. Then ladies . . . masks on. Let's start with En garde stance. The ready position.

MARIAM slams her mask down, and snaps into En garde. She's good. LAINIE reluctantly puts her mask on. She tries to copy MARIAM's stance.

(to LAINIE) Is it okay if I adjust your position?

LAINIE	Yeah.
CADDELL	Nice and low. Keep your balance.

He steps in and demos a stance, making sure LAINIE's solid on her feet. He steps back and looks at them both.

Good. This is where a fight starts. When both fighters are ready.

MARIAM	In fencing they fight clean.

LAINIE   What's that supposed to mean?—

CADDELL   —girls, c'mon. We haven't even made contact with the foils yet. Okay, a little closer . . . right there. You want to space yourselves so that your weapons are this far apart.

He shows them the distance with the swords. Held out, they are at a safe distance.

This fighting distance is your measure. That means it's safe. She can't reach you. You can't reach her. This is one of the most important things in stage fighting. More accidents occur because the fighters are too close together than any other reason.

Okay, let's try some footwork. Lainie, keeping your sword in this position, try to advance and retreat with your feet only. Quick, shuffling steps. Like this . . .

He demos.

You advance when you are attacking. Retreat when you're defending. Okay, Mariam, advance on Lainie. Lainie . . . retreat. And . . . go . . .

LAINIE doesn't want to retreat.

Lainie. Retreat means backwards.

LAINIE   Why do I have to retreat?

CADDELL   Because if you don't, it's really easy for her to do this.

He taps MARIAM's sword hand. She scores a hit on LAINIE's shoulder.

Keep your distance and you'll make it harder for her to score a point.

LAINIE   Fine.

CADDELL   And . . . go.

They go again. Grudgingly, LAINIE retreats.

Okay. That was harder than it needed to be. Back the other way. And . . . go.

They do. LAINIE likes this better. She's aggressive. Too fast. MARIAM backpedals quickly, but LAINIE scores an ugly hit on MARIAM's leg.

MARIAM   What the?

CADDELL   Whoa . . . whoa—

MARIAM   —you said we were just doing footwork!

CADDELL   That's right. I did—

MARIAM   —and these are foils. That's not even a target!

CADDELL   Okay . . . okay . . . everyone take a deep breath. Let's try advancing again, Lainie. *Just footwork* this time. Slowly. And . . . go.

LAINIE does a single slow advance. See?

Good.

A second one. Faster. With more aggression.

(warning) Good.

A third. Full out charge.

(stopping her) Okay. Okay. Okay . . . Let's try some thrusts and parries.

So, Lainie, when we're fencing we're aiming at different areas or targets. I like to think of them like quadrants.

He turns and points to the whiteboard where he's drawn a person's torso bisected with a cross creating four equal quadrants.

Imagine the person you're fighting has a cross in the centre of their torso. There are two targets or areas above the rib cage . . .

And two below . . .

Each attack has a corresponding parry or way to defend against it. Each type of weapon has a different numbering system for those parries, but to keep it simple we'll use the parries 1, 2, 3, and 4. *(demo-ing the supinated parries)* In fencing, we do them with our palm up.

(to MARIAM) Yes?

MARIAM   Basically.

CADDELL   Okay, Mariam, you're up. Lainie, watch my attacks.

He runs through them, demo-ing on MARIAM. She does the correct parries.

1, 2, 3, and 4.

Okay. Mariam, attack me. Lainie, watch the parries.

MARIAM beats CADDELL's foil and slowly runs the attacks. He demos the parries, calling out each move by its number. LAINIE watches.

Nice and simple. Okay, Lainie, you're in. En garde. Check your measure . . . Good. Okay . . . This is all going to happen in super slooooow motion. Ten per cent speed. I'll stand here so you can see the parries. Mariam, thrust 1. And . . . go.

MARIAM does. LAINIE parries.

Good. Mariam, thrust 2.

She does. CADDELL shows LAINIE the corresponding parry. She parries the thrust.

Now 3.

MARIAM thrusts to 3. LAINIE parries it.

4.

MARIAM thrusts to 4. LAINIE is starting to like it. It's getting faster and heavier.

Hey. You're way too heavy on the blade. Light. Light. Light. Control and finesse is what separates real fighters from the smashers and bashers. Softness is going to help you and make sure the blades stay connected. Not only does it make it safe . . . but you also get a cool sound . . .

He demos 1 through 4 again, then a big slide down MARIAM's foil. Nothing. They are stone-faced.

You're killing me here.

All right, fine. Drop the foils. Masks off. Let's try something else. C'mon. Get nice and close together and put your sword hand up like this.

He demos. They don't want to get close to each other.

C'mon. Closer.

Reluctantly, they do. He gets them to stand facing each other, with their elbows bent and their hands up in front of them, wrists touching. They are both tense.

Now relax. Nice soft hands.

This is where you always return to. It's like your En garde position. Don't let the contact between your wrists break. Now, Mariam, try to score a point on Lainie with your finger. Just a nice little *gentle* poke on the shoulder.

MARIAM quickly goes for LAINIE's right shoulder—target 3.

LAINIE   Hey.

Despite the speed, LAINIE naturally parries.

CADDELL   Yes!

LAINIE   That wasn't slow.

CADDELL   But did you feel that? That was a parry. Your instincts kicked in. You defended yourself. Good. Mariam, try another attack. Not so *fast* this time.

MARIAM tries another one. LAINIE parries again, too hard. But she gets her. Their animosity is palpable.

Soft . . . All right, Lainie, see if you can get a point.

She goes hard. MARIAM parries.

One more.

LAINIE makes a quick and aggressive attack. Way too hard. MARIAM does a double envelopment and tosses her hand to the side.

LAINIE   That's not fair!

23

MARIAM   You were going too hard.

LAINIE   He told me to get a point.

CADDELL   What she just did was an *envelopment*. It's a way of
            disarming your opponent.

LAINIE   She shouldn't have used it. You didn't teach me that
            one.

MARIAM   You were trying to punch me—

LAINIE   —I was not. / I was trying to *poke* you with my finger
            . . . just like he told me to.

MARIAM   / Yes, you were! You were trying to punch me—

CADDELL   —okay. Okay! Both of you need to work on being soft-
            er. Not only is softer faster . . .

He quickly scores a point on LAINIE.

            . . . but it gives you more control. As soon as you try
            and muscle it, like . . . uh . . .

He demos a heavy, muscled thrust. LAINIE *parries it easier.
She smiles. She gets it.*

            . . . you slow yourself down. Let's add foils and masks
            back in.

*The girls put their masks on, pick up their foils. Find distance.
En garde. As they do . . .*

            Now just imagine the energy between the swords is
            like the energy between your wrists. Got it?

They nod.

            Okay. Let's run the targets again . . . 1, 2, 3, and 4.

Mariam attacking. And . . . go.

MARIAM slowly advances on LAINIE, who retreats.

Good retreat. Keep the tension, Lainie. Good . . .

MARIAM runs through thrusts to 1, 2, 3, and 4.

Other way. Lainie, you attack.

LAINIE goes on the attack and starts the sequence going the other way, thrusting quickly to 1 and 2.

Easy . . .

MARIAM backpedals. LAINIE thrusts to 3 with a big advance. Too fast. Angry.

Arrêt!

MARIAM pulls up. LAINIE goes for a huge thrust to 4. MARIAM cringes, her foil and even her other arm up to protect herself.

Whoa! Back up! Tip down.

LAINIE finally stops, backs up.

MARIAM   Didn't you hear? He said stop.

LAINIE   No, he didn't.

MARIAM   *Arrêt!* means stop—

CADDELL slips in between them.

CADDELL   —in French. Sorry, I should have explained that at the beginning. Thank you, guys, you just taught me something pretty important. Remember to tell the students how to stop. And what *arrêt!* means.

LAINIE   We shouldn't have stopped. I almost scored a point.

MARIAM   We're not trying to score points. We're just / running through the targets—

LAINIE   / scared I might win?—

CADDELL   —Okay! More important than anything you two are arguing about . . . Lainie, your tip was way too high. Without a mask on you could have given Mariam an eye patch.

Now, before things got out of control, I was actually going to compliment you. You were working well together. Just . . . thought I would point that out.

The girls look at each other. Awkward.

Okay. You guys want to try a sequence? You're my guinea pigs, remember?

MARIAM rolls her eyes.

LAINIE   Sure.

CADDELL   Take your masks off. So for the top of the play, for that street fight I told you about, I'm going to need people from both families fighting. So let's say . . . Mariam, you're a Capulet. That's Juliet's family. Lainie, you'll be a Montague. Romeo's family. Your families have hated each other for generations. Now . . . you happen to run into each other in the street. What could happen that would start the fight? Any ideas? Two people don't just start fighting with swords in the middle of the street for no reason.

The girls think . . . Finally.

LAINIE   Well . . . if I was walking by I could spit. And maybe it gets close to her foot and she could get really pissed about that.

MARIAM   That's not realistic.

LAINIE   Are you kidding me? That happens in front of the downtown library ten times a day.[2]

MARIAM   People don't fight because of someone spitting.

LAINIE   Okay . . .

LAINIE walks by MARIAM, looking her in the eye. Stops in front of her and spits on the floor near her foot.

MARIAM   *(incredulous)* Shit. You almost hit me.

LAINIE   What are you going to do about it?

She walks up to MARIAM. MARIAM is livid.

                See? Now all I have to do is push you . . . we're in a fight.

CADDELL steps between them.

CADDELL   You know this territory pretty well.

LAINIE   *(shrugs)* I have brothers.

CADDELL   That's actually pretty good. Let's try it again. This time, Mariam, stand here. Lainie, start over there. Also, pretend your foil is in your belt, just hold it like this . . . *(He demos.)* because as young men you wouldn't go anywhere without them. *(to LAINIE)* Oh . . . and just *pretend* to spit this time.

---

2   Can be updated to local reference in your community where youth congregate.

MARIAM   Yeah. Try to control yourself.

LAINIE   *(taunting)* Wait and see. Wait and see . . . not sure if I can.

They get set. LAINIE saunters up to MARIAM. Stops in front of her and makes a big gesture to spit again. With a patronizing look, LAINIE pretends to spit. They look at each other. Real tension.

CADDELL   Good. Mariam, take a step towards her. Lainie . . . slowly put your hand on your foil.

She does. Pulls her foil out slightly, like she's showing a gun. Taunts MARIAM.

           (laughing) I think you've been watching too many movies. Okay. Mariam. Your character is getting mad. She wants a fight, you're ready.

MARIAM gets into En garde.

           Lainie. Now what about your character? She's a Montague.

LAINIE   She's not going to back down.

CADDELL   Okay then.

She gets into En garde.

           We've built all the little moments that lead up to the fight. Now let me give you some moves. I'll be you, Mariam.

He steps in to face LAINIE. He teaches them a very short piece of choreography. Two to three moves. MARIAM watches intently.

           En garde. Mariam, beat. *(demos a beat on LAINIE's foil)*

Thrust 4. *(He thrusts to* LAINIE's *4. She parries.)*

Lainie, thrust 4 back with an advance. *(LAINIE thrusts to his 4 with a step.)*

Expel her blade. *(He expels* LAINIE's *blade.)* Which means she's throwing it away. Big lunge forward. *(He lunges towards* LAINIE.*)*

Big retreat back. *(LAINIE retreats back.)*

Parry 2. *(He thrusts to* LAINIE's *2. She parries it.)*

And recover. *(They go back to En garde.)*

Okay, you try.

MARIAM jumps in, keen to try.

Ten per cent speed.

She has picked it up. They do it over and over with CADDELL *calling out moves and corrections. They are intensely focused.*

Okay. Forty per cent speed.

Okay. Seventy per cent. And recover.

They stop and return to En garde.

Great! Let's run the whole thing. Run through the scene until the moment you draw your swords.

Now this is crucial. We're gonna pause right at that moment, and I want you to look at each other. This moment of eye contact is built into every fight. Why?

MARIAM   So you know the other person is ready?

LAINIE   But when you're fighting someone, it's better if they don't see it coming.

CADDELL   But see . . . that's the big difference between a real fight and a stage fight. Onstage, you're working *with* your partner like a dance, not against them. You start before the other person's ready, someone's gonna get hurt for real.

Okay. Once you pause don't start until I say go . . . Lainie, walk by Mariam.

The girls run the top of the scene. As they get to the beginning of the fight, they pause and look at each other.

Go.

They run the fight sequence. Best ever. It's starting to look like a real fight.

Arrêt!

They both stop.

Fantastic. I can totally use that sequence in the opening. All right, let's take a break. I gotta write some of this down.

Both girls are sweating. They've been working hard. CADDELL *exits. Without him there, suddenly it's awkward again.* MARIAM *crosses away and sits on one side of the space.* LAINIE *sits on the other.*

CADDELL *re-enters with a notebook, some bottles of water, and a bag of chips. He notices the distance between them.*

I don't know about you. But fighting always makes me hungry.

He tosses them both a bottled water. Opens the bag of chips.

Passes it to them.

> *(to MARIAM)* How long have you been fencing?

MARIAM Junior high.

CADDELL Cool. I don't know many people your age who fence.

MARIAM Most of the people at my club are university students. Or, like . . . adults.

CADDELL Hunh.

LAINIE rolls her eyes. She thinks MARIAM's bragging. MARIAM notices. CADDELL feels the tension in the air. He grabs the chips. Tosses them to LAINIE.

> *(to LAINIE)* You did well considering you've never held a foil before.

LAINIE throws him a look.

> I'm serious. It's not easy to learn. It's not like we handle swords every day.

She shrugs. CADDELL grabs his notebook. Starts to write down the fight.

> Good thing we did this today. You actually picked up things way faster than I thought you would. Another note for myself . . . make sure to have extra stuff prepared when I come in to work with the cast in case they're as quick as you.

LAINIE watches him.

LAINIE If you like fighting so much, why do you want to be a teacher?

CADDELL Why?

LAINIE   Yeah, like if you're so good at this. And at acting, why
            don't you move to Hollywood? Or Toronto[3] at least.

CADDELL   Ah. The age-old question.

LAINIE   I mean being a teacher sucks . . .

CADDELL   Why do you say that?

LAINIE   You have to deal with kids who like, don't want to be
            at school. Who don't want to listen to you. That total-
            ly blow you off. That pretty much has to suck.

CADDELL   I imagine it could.

LAINIE   Or, you have to put up with the other end. Kids who
            just want to hang out with you all the time . . . total
            brown-nosers . . . no life of their own. That'll drive you
            nuts.

CADDELL   That could be challenging.

LAINIE   And we don't know how to do stuff . . . isn't that super
            frustrating?

CADDELL   Well, I guess it could be if you let it.

            But . . . you could look at it another way . . . like, you
            get to work with young people when they're just fig-
            uring out who they are, and what they want to do,
            and what matters to them . . . And I don't know . . .
            that's kind of amazing.

LAINIE   That's lame.

CADDELL   Seriously. Maybe I've been lucky but I've had a few
            great teachers that ignited something in me. I don't

---

3   This reference can be updated if necessary to the city perceived to be
    the place to be an actor.

know how they did it, but they got through to me. They taught me stuff I'll remember for the rest of my life.

MARIAM   Like your fight teacher?

CADDELL   Definitely. I've actually been fortunate enough to learn from a few different teachers. Working with them changed me.

He turns to LAINIE.

So . . . I don't know if that answers your question, but I guess that's why . . . I want to do what they did for me. Do what I love, but more than that. Pass it along.

LAINIE rolls her eyes.

Look, it's not that I didn't want to be an actor. That was my original plan. Act professionally. Maybe even fight professionally.

But . . . you know what I realized when I got out of school? There are a lot of good actors out there. There are even a lot of good fighters out there. But you know what there aren't a lot of? Good actors who are good fighters . . . who are good teachers.

On a good day . . . I *think* I can do all three. I hope I can.

MARIAM   You're okay.

CADDELL is surprised. He turns to her.

As a teacher.

CADDELL   Thanks.

MARIAM   I mean. You got us to do a fight already. It's not even lunch.

CADDELL   And no injuries so far. Perfect track record. *(to LAINIE)* Although I was a little worried when you almost spit on Mariam's shoe.

The girls look at each other. Almost smile.

           All right. Enough lazing around. Who wants to learn some unarmed? Hand to hand . . .

MARIAM   It's *Romeo and Juliet*. Shakespeare? Everyone fights with swords.

CADDELL   Not all the fighting in the play happens that way.

           Violence is actually woven all through the script. It's in the big sword fights for sure. But . . . he also wrote violence into places you wouldn't expect. Like some of the scenes between Juliet, her dad, her mom, and the Nurse.

MARIAM   I guess.

CADDELL   I've worked on the play a couple of times . . . and I don't know . . . the more I work on it, the more I think Shakespeare was trying to use the story to talk about how violence touches all aspects of our lives. To show how it touches us as children. As parents. As friends. And in the bigger picture . . . as a community.

Beat.

           So . . . Let's start with a simple throw and fall. The skills you need to do this are base concepts for lots of other unarmed moves. That sound good?

LAINIE   *(keen)* Sure.

MARIAM   *(unsure)* I guess.

CADDELL   Lainie, let's start with you throwing me.

LAINIE steps up.

> Grab the front of my shirt . . . it's all right. Go for it.

She does.

> Is it cool if I hold on to your forearms?

She nods. He holds on to LAINIE's forearms.

> You always want to hang on to something meaty . . .

She looks at him. Indignant.

> I'm just saying . . . it's way easier to hurt someone hanging onto a wrist or an elbow.

> Now, here's the thing to remember. Unlike in real life, the person throwing isn't the one in control. The victim is. So, Lainie, your job is to *pretend* to really wind up and throw me, but I'm actually going to do all the work. Got it?

LAINIE   I guess.

CADDELL   Okay, let's try this nice and slow. Lainie . . . pull me back . . . and throw me.

She does it. CADDELL falls backwards, gracefully onto the floor. He jumps up.

> Good. Now to fall safely, I just did a couple of things. First, I got my bum down nice and low, so I don't have far to fall. I also had my one leg out to help me balance.

Now, as I slowly fall backwards . . . this is critical. I kept my arms forward. Like I was going to tie my shoe.

Arms back . . . hospital. Broken wrists. No snowboarding.[4] Arms forward . . . no hospital. Happy. Can play video games.[5] *(He demos again.)* Hospital. No hospital. Hospital. No hospital. Got it?

And here I go.

With LAINIE's *help, he completes a second fall. Nice and smooth.*

Mariam, jump in here. Let's have you try one with Lainie.

MARIAM *reluctantly steps up. The two girls are closer together than they've been since the fight. They're uncomfortable. This is a little too familiar.*

Okay, Lainie, start by taking Mariam by the shirt. Mariam, you're okay with that?

MARIAM   Yeah.

LAINIE *steps in and takes two handfuls of the front of* MARIAM's *shirt, up near her collar.*

CADDELL   Good. So the first step is eye contact. That's the cue.

They look at each other. This is hard.

Second step. The pullback. Nice and slow. Good. Nice . . . And now the throw.

---

4   Can replace snowboarding with another reference to something desirable she would want to do that requires hands and wrists.

5   Can can replace video games with another reference to something desirable she would want to do that requires her hands and wrists.

LAINIE throws her. MARIAM begins to fall. She's awkward. Not sure what to do with her hands.

Good . . .

MARIAM   Ugh. It's so awkward.

CADDELL   Not bad. Keep your arms forward though. Remember . . . Hospital. No hospital.

Okay, let's reverse. Mariam, throw Lainie.

MARIAM takes LAINIE by the shirt. Lightly pulls her back. Throws her. LAINIE does a dramatic fall back. She's pretty good, but way too much energy.

Whoa. Good arms. Didn't entirely make sense with the throw Mariam gave you, but we'll work on that.

LAINIE   What do you mean? It was good.

CADDELL   It *was* good. But we have to make sure the reaction matches the action. Here, I'll show you. Mariam, throw me.

MARIAM does another wimpy throw. CADDELL throws himself back in a huge fall, doing a hard knap on the floor. It sounds like he's broken his tailbone. The girls are shocked.

Guys . . . that's called acting.

LAINIE   That was awesome!

CADDELL   Ah. It was dramatic. It was loud. But was it realistic?

LAINIE   Well . . . I guess not really. Mariam didn't throw you very hard.

MARIAM throws her a look. Oh really.

CADDELL   Exactly. An audience isn't going to believe it if the reaction doesn't match the action. It looks fake.

LAINIE   It happens in movies all the time. A guy punches another guy and he goes flying. That's not what really happens.

CADDELL   No kidding.

LAINIE   Also, if you really punch someone, your hand hurts for like a week.

MARIAM   *(quietly)* You would know.

LAINIE   *(turning on her)* Sorry if I know how to punch someone. Not everyone gets driven to the university to learn fencing. Some of us have to live in the real world.

CADDELL   Look. Here's the thing about stage fighting. It isn't the real world. But it helps to know what things really feel like, so we can make it look realistic for the audience.

Beat.

Okay. That was a good start. Let's move on and learn a punch. Lainie, you seem to know a lot about action movies. You up for this? *(She nods.)* Okay, we stand nice and close like we did for the throw and fall. My fist comes from my shoulder, across your body, underneath your chin in a direct line. My measure or fighting distance for this move is at least eight inches away from your body.

He demos with LAINIE. *She turns her face. She's on top of it.*

MARIAM   That looks totally fake.

CADDELL   Hold on. That's because we're showing it from the wrong angle so you can see how it's done.

Okay, just for now, Mariam, come sit over here and pretend you're the audience. Let's imagine that the audience is sitting right there from here to here . . .

He puts his arms in a V, to indicate where. It's exactly where the real audience is sitting. MARIAM sits in the middle, right in front of the first row.

This is their sightline, what they can see when they look at the stage. Now, let me know if this looks more realistic.

He gets LAINIE to put her back to the audience. He sets up a stacked punch.

(to LAINIE) Nothing's going to change. Let's do exactly what we did.

He runs through it slowly, then he punches her. With a knap on his chest. It looks real. He looks back at MARIAM.

MARIAM   *(surprised)* Whoa . . . that was way better.

CADDELL   Turning the punch so that the action is hidden by our bodies makes all the difference. The knap helps sell it too. The knap's the sound that I'm making on my chest.

He demos a few more knaps.

It really helps us believe I'm making contact.

With a little acting, we can make this even more convincing. Lainie, you're already turning your head, which is great. This time can you make a sound? I mean, a punch that hard would really hurt right?

LAINIE   Oh yeah.

They do it again. LAINIE lets out a painful grunt as she's punched. It's even better.

MARIAM   That was better.

CADDELL   This time, after you get punched and let out that sound, let this hand come up and grab your jaw. I mean, it's killing you, right? And I'm going to take what you said earlier, Lainie, and really play how much it hurts *me*.

They do it again. This time CADDELL nurses his sore hand. Groaning.

             What do you think?

MARIAM   *(impressed)* Oooh. It looks pretty real.

CADDELL   So the sightlines, or which angle the people see the fight from, are so important, right? Otherwise it wouldn't work. It would look fake.

MARIAM   Kind of like a magic trick.

CADDELL   Exactly. What sold it to the audience was our acting. What it felt like for me to do it. What Lainie felt as she got hit. Hurt. A little scared maybe. The emotions of it.

MARIAM is thinking about their own fight. So is LAINIE. They look at each other.

LAINIE   Yeah.

CADDELL   Okay. Hair pull. This is a fun one. There are a couple of ways to do it, but it's all victim control.

He indicates for them to come and join him. They do, one on each side of him.

> First way is I move to grab your hair but close my fist before I catch any and just place my fist on the top of your head.

He demos this on MARIAM.

> Mariam, you grab my fist as if you're trying to get me to let go, but actually just hold my hand to your head. Good! That's it. Then you're completely in control.
>
> The other way is to slide my open hand into your hair and rest it on the back of your head.

While still hanging on to MARIAM, *he slides his hand into* LAINIE's *hair.*

> *(to* LAINIE) Now, same thing, hang on to my hand as if you're trying to get me to let go.

She does.

> Now you're completely in control.
>
> Now . . . go for it, move around like I have both of you by the hair!

They do. He shakes them like two puppies. In spite of themselves, they're laughing.

> Add in some acting. Let's hear some noise.

They both grunt quietly. Self conscious. Not believable.

> C'mon. Go for it!

They do.

Fantastic.

He lets go, giving them each a noogie as he does.

Wow. You both need some help in the hair department.

Their hair is a mess. They straighten themselves up. They're having fun.

All right. One last one. The slap.

MARIAM   I don't remember a slap in *Romeo and Juliet*.

CADDELL   Sadly, this is one of the most common unarmed moves used in this play against women.

He goes and grabs his script out of his bag. It's a well-loved copy.

There is a scene in Act III . . . yeah, here it is. Scene 5, where the slap usually happens. It's the scene where Romeo and Juliet have just been secretly married and they've spent the night together. Romeo has been banished by the Prince and they both know if anyone finds him in Verona, he'll be killed.

LAINIE   So he takes off.

CADDELL   Yep. Good thing too, because just then, Juliet's mom comes in. She's completely distraught that her nephew has been killed and she swears vengeance on the man who killed him.

LAINIE   Romeo.

MARIAM   I thought you didn't read it.

LAINIE   I didn't. I remember that part from the movie.

CADDELL   Then Juliet's mom drops a bomb. The real reason she's come to her room. Juliet's father has decided that she must marry a young rich lord . . . Paris.

MARIAM   She can't.

CADDELL   Exactly. She's already married to Romeo. So she refuses. Her mom is furious . . . and, I always think, kind of scared of how her husband is going to react. She says . . .

Here comes your father; tell him so yourself,
And see how he will take it at your hands.

LAINIE   And lemme guess . . . Dad shows up. And goes ballistic.

CADDELL   Absolutely. He threatens her. He says:

Thank me no thankings, nor, proud me no prouds,
But fettle your fine joints 'gainst Thursday next,
To go with Paris to Saint Peter's Church,
Or I will drag thee on a hurdle thither.

MARIAM   A hurdle?

CADDELL   Not like a track and field hurdle . . . in Shakespeare's day, a hurdle was kind of like a . . . well, almost like a sleigh that they dragged prisoners down the street on when they were going to execute them.

MARIAM   But she's his daughter. And isn't she like fourteen?

CADDELL   Yeah. But that doesn't stop him. He starts yelling at her. Calling her names.

MARIAM   Nobody says anything?

CADDELL   Ah . . . now see, that's the moment her mom finally steps in. He's a violent man, but finally she can't take it and she says:

Fie, fie! what, are you mad?

And this is the spot where many professional productions have Lord Capulet slap his wife across the face.

MARIAM   That's horrible.

CADDELL   It is. A slap is one of the most private, intimate acts of violence you can do to another person. He does it to stop her from interfering. But in a way, he also uses that violence to threaten his daughter. By hitting his wife, he's saying if you don't do what I want, I'll hurt your mom, this person that you love.

LAINIE   Or I'll hurt you.

CADDELL   Yeah. It's a warning.

           With Lord Capulet, Shakespeare has created a character that's hard for us to grapple with. In many ways, he's a monstrous, violent man, but he's still her dad and she has always been protected from this side of him by her mom and the Nurse. Finally in this moment, she sees his true nature.

MARIAM   He's a bully.

CADDELL   Someone who uses violence to force people to do what he wants. He uses violence as a weapon.

           So . . . Juliet is horrified by this, and scared for her mother, but she tries to reason with him. This is the final straw. He says:

           Speak not, reply not, do not answer me.
           My fingers itch.

MARIAM   ·He threatens to hit his own kid?

CADDELL   Absolutely. "My fingers itch" . . . that's what he's saying.

MARIAM   What happens next?

CADDELL   He tells Juliet that if she doesn't marry Paris, he will kick her out and let her starve in the street and that no one in the family will ever be allowed to see her.

Silence. They all think.

   Everyone thinks *Romeo and Juliet* is just a love story. But in many ways, it's a story about violence.

LAINIE   And how messed up families can get.

CADDELL   Yeah.

   It's always a little strange staging fights. Because in a way, it's fun to learn stage combat. Like today. We kind of had fun right?

LAINIE   . . . Yeah.

CADDELL   And that's the thing. It's normal that people find it fun to figure out how to do all this stuff . . . It's fun because we're doing it safely and no one's getting hurt. But it's important to remember . . . we're actually learning how to do these moves because we need to be able to show dark, violent, awful moments onstage. Playwrights craft these moments because they have something to say about violence.

   Our job as stage fighters is to make those moments clear.

Pause. They're all thinking. CADDELL *looks at his watch.*

Okay. So usually what I do now is have my students choreograph their own short fight scene using all these unarmed moves . . . But you know what? It's lunchtime. You guys have put in some serious work today. I think we're good. Let's call it a day.

LAINIE   That's it?

CADDELL   Yeah. You really held up your side. You showed up. You did your time. You helped me figure some stuff out. You're off the hook. Can you girls grab the mat?

He goes and starts to clear up his stuff. The girls look at each other. They don't really want to quit. They slowly put the mat away.

LAINIE   There isn't anything else you need to practise? There were a lot of sword fights in the movie.

MARIAM   *(discouraged)* He doesn't need girls for those big fights. Only guys do those in the play.

CADDELL looks at her.

All Shakespeare's plays are like that.

When we read *Hamlet*, the girls just killed themselves or drank poison and died.

LAINIE   That's what you told us happens in *Romeo and Juliet* too. The mom and the Nurse get slapped and thrown around and then Juliet kills herself with a stupid little knife. The girls don't get to do anything cool. It's crap!

CADDELL   Hey . . . Everyone's gonna get something cool to do.

LAINIE   *(disappointed)* Yeah. Sure.

MARIAM   Whatever.

CADDELL   Thanks for coming.

They exit. CADDELL *watches them go. He goes to pick up* LAIN-IE'*s mask. Looks at it. Thinks for a moment. Puts it in his bag.*

Shift.

He turns out to us. He's talking to Mrs. Lee.

> Mrs. Lee . . . um . . . do you have a minute? I'm sorry to bug you. I know you've got your hands full . . . yikes . . . journals . . .
>
> The thing is . . . I was wondering if you had finalized the casting yet. I . . . don't want to step on your toes, I mean, you know the kids way better than I do, but . . . it just sort of hit me the other day. It's kind of unfair that so many women in Shakespeare's plays only get to be thrown down or hurt, or kill themselves . . . but never get to do any of the big sword fights. Working with Mariam and Lainie—and seeing how much more confidence they're gaining . . . I was just wondering . . .
>
> Well, I was wondering if you might consider casting them in some of the fighting roles. *(listens)* Yeah, I can see how it might be a little controversial to cast a girl as Romeo, but . . . what about Mercutio? That could work. And Tybalt, you know, that could be a really interesting twist.
>
> . . . So . . . anyhow . . . I know they're huge parts. Big challenges. But I think they can do it.
>
> It's just a suggestion.
>
> It's your call.

Shift.

It's Monday. The girls appear.

LAINIE Mrs. Lee said you wanted to see us?

CADDELL Yeah.

He looks disappointed.

> There's just something I needed to say to you two. I wanted you to know, I really heard what you both said on Saturday. About girls, and the fighting parts and everything. So . . . I talked to Mrs. Lee. I *tried* to get her to understand . . .

The girls are confused. What now?

> And she did.

He grabs a script out of his bag. Tosses it to LAINIE.

> You're playing Mercutio.

He tosses another one to MARIAM.

> You're Tybalt.

LAINIE *(shocked)* What?

MARIAM In the play?

CADDELL Last time I checked.

LAINIE Are you kidding me?

MARIAM But they're *guys*?

CADDELL I know. But a couple of people said to me once . . . wouldn't it be cool, if for once, the girls got the swords? If they got the big fight?

48

LAINIE   The big fight?

CADDELL   Mercutio and Tybalt have a huge faceoff, then Romeo takes on Tybalt. It's massive.

LAINIE   Holy crap.

CADDELL   And we're not using foils. We're going to use sabres. So we don't need these anymore. *(He indicates the foils.)* Lainie, can you take these to Mrs. Lee's office? She knows where they get locked up . . . and Lainie? I know it's tempting, but don't take them out of the bag, okay?

LAINIE   Okay.

She picks up the bag and runs off. MARIAM *just sits there.* CADDELL *sits down next to her. He smiles.*

CADDELL   Sabres . . . pretty cool, hunh?

She doesn't say anything.

I thought you'd be happy.

MARIAM   . . . I am . . .

CADDELL   . . . but . . .

MARIAM   I'm just . . .

CADDELL   What?

MARIAM   Nothing.

CADDELL   Hey . . . this stuff between you and Lainie . . . you're working it out. I know it's hard . . . but it's going to be okay.

MARIAM   It's not that.

Finally.

I . . . I've never been in a play before.

CADDELL *didn't see this coming.*

CADDELL   But . . . you're part of the drama club.

MARIAM   Yeah.

CADDELL   Well, I guess I just assumed you've done some productions.

MARIAM   I have. It's just . . . I was the stage manager.

CADDELL   Oh.

LAINIE *is back. In the doorway.*

LAINIE   Don't worry about it. You know how to fence.

MARIAM *looks at her.* LAINIE *wasn't supposed to hear that.*

You're way ahead of me. I've only been in one play, and it was a crappy part. I didn't even have any lines—

MARIAM   *(sharp)* —this isn't about you.

LAINIE   Why are you biting my head off? / Don't you get it? I'm trying to tell you you're going to be good—

MARIAM   / Because I don't need your pity. I don't care what you think of me—

LAINIE   What's your problem?

MARIAM   Shut up—

CADDELL   —hey! I went to bat for you two. We're not going there again.

For what it's worth. Lainie's right, Mariam. Tybalt's an amazing part. He's the best fighter in the play. All the other characters say so.

What do you say? You in?

The girls stare at each other.

LAINIE   *(quietly, almost a taunt)* C'mon, Mariam . . . *fight* me.

Beat. Finally.

MARIAM   Fine.

CADDELL   Okay.

You have your scripts. Start reading the scenes you're in. We start tomorrow after school. I've booked the theatre. We're going to start building the fight right away. Four o'clock?

LAINIE   Sure.

MARIAM nods.

CADDELL   See you there.

He exits. The two girls look at each other. Tension. Real tension. LAINIE turns abruptly and exits.

Shift.

MARIAM is alone. In her own area. She opens her script.

MARIAM   *(reads)* Act I, Scene 5.

She skims through the scene.

(to herself) Okay . . . Romeo first meets Juliet at the

Capulet's party. He's wearing a mask, but Tybalt recognizes him.

She tries to take on what she imagines Tybalt is like.

Tybalt.

(reads) This, by his voice, should be a Montague. . . . What dares the slave come hither . . .

(She reads ahead.) I guess I must go for him . . . because Lord Capulet stops me.

A voice:

LORD
CAPULET   *Why, how now, kinsman! Wherefore storm you so?*

MARIAM   *Uncle, this is a Montague, our foe,*

LORD
CAPULET   *Young Romeo is it?*

MARIAM   *'Tis he, that villain Romeo.*
                 . . . I'll not endure him.

LORD
CAPULET   *He shall be endured:*

MARIAM, as TYBALT, sighs. Bows. LORD CAPULET is gone. She looks out at the audience and reads.

MARIAM   *I will withdraw.*

She looks across the stage, where she, and we, see LAINIE appear. Also alone with her script. She opens it.

LAINIE   *(reads)* Act II. Scene 3. Enter Benvolio and Mercutio. *(to herself)* Benvolio is his friend . . . okay . . .

She tries taking on the physicality of a guy. Mercutio.

> *(reads) Where the devil should this Romeo be?*
> *Came he not home to-night?*

A voice:

BENVOLIO   *Not to his father's; I spoke with his man . . .*
Tybalt, the kinsman of old Capulet,
Hath sent a letter to his father's house.

LAINIE   *A challenge, on my life.*

BENVOLIO   *Romeo will answer it.*

LAINIE   *Any man that can write may answer a letter.*
. . . is he a man to encounter Tybalt?

BENVOLIO   *Why, what is Tybalt?*

LAINIE looks over at MARIAM.

LAINIE   *More than prince of cats, I can tell you. He fights as*
you sing prick-song, rests me his minim rest, one,
two, and the third in your bosom:

Using her pencil, she acts out what she reads. Ends with a
thrust in MARIAM's direction.

> Ha!

> *A duellist . . . a duellist . . .*

The girls stare at each other.

Shift.

They toss their scripts down. Cross into the centre, and begin
to fight. Vicious. Messy. CADDELL enters.

CADDELL   What the— Stop . . . Stop!

He pulls them apart.

LAINIE   What?

MARIAM   We're *practising*.

CADDELL   What?

LAINIE   We know you want to save the unarmed for the other scene but you told us that you usually get people to make up their own fight.

MARIAM   So we did.

LAINIE   We don't want to suck in front of the whole school. Wait a minute. *(realizing)* You thought we were really fighting? *(to MARIAM)* Ooh . . . it must have looked good.

He sits down.

MARIAM   Are you okay?

CADDELL   I think I just saw my future teaching certificate flash before my eyes.

He looks at them. Shakes his head.

(honestly) Girls . . . that was great.

They look at each other. A small moment of pride.

Okay, before we tackle any lines, let's look at the differences between foils and the weapons we're going to be using for the play . . . sabres.

He pulls a sabre out of the case. It's impressive.

These are bladed weapons, so they are for cutting . . . as well as thrusting.

That means our parries are going to be a little different, knuckles up, and we're adding a new target—the head. But don't worry. We have plenty of time before opening night to drill and rehearse. So grab a sabre and a belt. Grab your scripts. Let's build the scene.

Romeo and Juliet. Act III. Scene 1.

(reads) Enter Mercutio and Benvolio. *(to LAINIE and MARIAM)* All right . . . I'll play Benvolio. Let's just walk through it and see what we discover, okay, Lainie. So the scene starts with us walking down a street in Verona.

I pray thee, good Mercutio, let's retire:
The day is hot, the Capulets abroad,
And, if we meet, we shall not scape a brawl;.

LAINIE *(reads) Thou art like one of those fellows that when he enters the confines of a tavern claps me his sword upon the table and says 'God send me no need of thee!' and by the operation of the second cup draws it on the drawer, when indeed there is no need.*

CADDELL Do you know what that means?

LAINIE Uh . . . I think I'm kinda saying you're like a guy who gets to the bar and says he's just there to drink. But by the time he has his second beer he's attacking you and you're his friend.

CADDELL Yep, that's pretty much it.

All right. Back to the scene. *Am I like such a fellow?*

LAINIE *(awkwardly) Thou!*

CADDELL   Hang on . . . I know we think of "thou" as a fancy word, but "thou" is just like saying "you" . . . *Am I like such a fellow?*

LAINIE   *Thou! why,*
thou wilt quarrel with a man for cracking nuts,
having no other reason but because thou hast hazel eyes . . .
. . . and yet thou wilt tutor me from quarrelling!

She's starting to really get into it.

CADDELL   *(impressed)* Good.

LAINIE   I actually kind of get what I'm saying.

CADDELL   I can tell.

LAINIE   I like Mercutio. He's kind of a smartass.

CADDELL   Exactly! So we're joking around about how much we like to fight when in comes Tybalt. Mariam, enter with confidence.

MARIAM saunters over.

By my head, here come the Capulets.

LAINIE   *(pushing him aside) By my heel, I care not.*

CADDELL   Good. *(gently)* Okay, Mariam. Tybalt has something to say.

MARIAM   *Gentlemen, good den . . .* den?

CADDELL   Good den is just an old-fashioned way to say "good day."

MARIAM   *. . . good den; a word with one of you.*

LAINIE *And but one word with one of us? Couple it with something; make it a word and a blow.*

MARIAM *Mercutio, thou consort'st* . . . consortest? . . .

CADDELL Yep. That's how you say it. *Consortest* . . . it means "hangs out" . . . Keep going!

MARIAM *thou consort'st with Romeo—*

LAINIE *Consort! What, dost thou make us minstrels? an thou make minstrels of us, look to hear nothing but discords: here's my fiddlestick;*

CADDELL Whoa . . . whoa . . . what's he talking about?

LAINIE I have no idea.

CADDELL His *fiddlestick?* His sword. Draw your sword on the line. Keep reading . . . it'll make sense.

LAINIE Okay . . . *here's my fiddlestick;*

She pulls out her sword. She looks at it. She's getting it.

Ah . . .

here's that shall make you dance. 'Zounds? . . . consort!

CADDELL 'Zounds is like "How dare you . . . "

LAINIE Oh . . . I get it. *'Zounds, consort!*

CADDELL Good. You really want to fight. But I try to calm you down.

We talk here in the public haunt of men:
Either withdraw unto some private place,
Or else depart; here all eyes gaze on us.

57

Remember, the Prince warned them that anybody caught fighting in the street will be put to death. What do you say?

LAINIE stares at MARIAM.

LAINIE   *Men's eyes were made to look, and let them gaze;*
I will not budge for no man's pleasure, I.

CADDELL   Mercutio would challenge Tybalt to a fight right now, except what does Shakespeare do? He sends Romeo in. Okay . . . I'll be Romeo. So he enters . . .

MARIAM   *Well, peace be with you, sir: here comes my man.*

CADDELL   Exactly. The guy he really wants to fight is Romeo.

MARIAM   *Romeo, the love I bear thee can afford*
No better term than this,—thou art a villain.

I don't get it. Why do I say I love him? And then call him a villain?

CADDELL   I think Tybalt's being sarcastic. Making fun of him to see if he can get him to fight. Try it again . . .

MARIAM   *Romeo, the "love" I bear thee can afford*
No better term than this,—thou art a villain.

CADDELL   Good. But Romeo doesn't rise to the challenge does he? Who has he just married in secret?

MARIAM   Juliet.

CADDELL   Exactly. So Tybalt, who is Juliet's cousin, is now his kinsmen . . . part of his family . . . so instead Romeo says:

Tybalt, the reason that I have to love thee
Doth much excuse the appertaining rage

To such a greeting: villain am I none;
Therefore farewell.

And Romeo tries to walk away. But does that work?

MARIAM   No. I say . . .

Boy, this shall not excuse the injuries
That thou hast done me; therefore turn and draw.

(realizing) Draw means pull out your sword.

CADDELL   Exactly.

MARIAM   So he's daring Romeo to fight him.

CADDELL   Exactly! But instead Romeo says:

I do protest, I never injured thee,
But love thee better than thou canst devise,
And so, good Capulet,—which name I tender
As dearly as my own,—be satisfied.

And he walks away.

In a different play, this would be the end. But Shake-speare has made Mercutio proud. For Mercutio, Romeo walking away is the biggest insult ever.

LAINIE   I get that. You walk away, you lose face. People don't respect you.

CADDELL   So what does he do?

LAINIE   I yell at Romeo . . . *O calm, dishonourable, vile sub-mission!*

Tybalt, you rat-catcher, will you walk? (to CADDELL*)* Walk?

CADDELL   Fight!

MARIAM   *What wouldst thou have with me?*

LAINIE   *Good king of cats, nothing but one of your nine lives; Will you pluck your sword out of his . . . pilcher?*

CADDELL   Scabbard!

LAINIE   *. . . pilcher by the ears? make haste, lest mine be about your ears ere it be out.*

MARIAM   *I am for you.*

CADDELL   Then what does it say. The stage direction.

MARIAM   *(She reads.) They fight.*

CADDELL   That's how the fight starts.

LAINIE   That's how all fights start.

CADDELL   What do you mean?

LAINIE   Smack talk, then a lot of beaking off, but then something always happens. There's always this moment. When nothing can stop it. They're gonna fight.

CADDELL   *(quietly)* See . . . that's why this scene is so famous. Because Shakespeare captured something completely real. It doesn't matter that he wrote it in the 1500s. Everyone who's been in a fight recognizes that moment. How it starts.

MARIAM   But why can't Romeo just tell him the truth?

CADDELL   Because the truth is complicated. And people are complicated.

We don't always tell each other what's going on. And we can't always know. Even if people tell us, we can never really know the whole story. In their heads, in their families, at home, with their friends, at school.

We might think we know, but honestly . . . we have no idea . . .

The girls look at each other.

MARIAM Yeah.

CADDELL So this is how we get to "the fight."

It's a vicious fight. Romeo is desperate and gets between them to stop them, and Mercutio is stabbed in the process. Mercutio, Romeo's dearest friend, dies in his arms.

LAINIE Mercutio dies?

CADDELL Absolutely.

LAINIE —wait a minute. Mercutio's a really good fighter. There's no way he could lose.

CADDELL Well he does. If he doesn't, the rest of the story doesn't happen and it becomes a romantic comedy. *When Romeo Met Juliet.*

LAINIE But—

CADDELL —Lainie, listen. Sometimes in drama . . . somebody has to die.

LAINIE Why?

CADDELL Because in that split second, where Romeo is holding your body and then Tybalt comes back in, Romeo doesn't see Tybalt as his cousin, his kinsman anymore . . . all he sees is the man who killed his best friend. He goes at Tybalt in a white rage, and despite Tybalt's incredible fighting skills, Romeo kills him.

MARIAM   Wait a minute . . . I die too?

CADDELL   Has anybody other than me read the play?

Okay. This is probably the second most important thing that happens. Romeo kills Tybalt. Why is it so important? It's the turning point. In that terrible moment, he realizes truly what he has done. He has just committed a crime, murdered someone, for which he will never be forgiven by the Capulets. Any hope of a happy life with Juliet is gone. And this act . . . killing Tybalt is what sets the tragedy of the play into motion. Which eventually leads to the deaths of both Romeo and Juliet.

LAINIE   So . . . we both have to die.

CADDELL   Yes, for the story to happen, the tragedy to unfold . . . you both have to die.

Okay, let's take a little break. Grab some water. And then let's figure out how this fight, and both your *deaths*, go together.

They nod. They exit.

Shift.

CADDELL look out at us. Shakes his head.

The funny thing is, I woke up this morning and thought to myself . . . opening night. Usually I'm happy to get to opening because it means that all the rehearsing is done and we can finally just do the show. Perform for an audience.

But this morning . . . I don't know . . . I felt different. It's not that I'm not happy, it's just . . . in a weird way I'm sad to see rehearsals end. I mean, don't get me wrong, the girls are ready, they're going to do a great job tonight. I think their families, their friends are going to love the show . . . but my job is done. And I wish it wasn't.

The girls enter. They are in costume, ready for opening, and extremely nervous. MARIAM *looks like she is going to throw up.*

Wow. You look great. You get my cards?

LAINIE   Yeah, but why did you tell us to *break a leg*?

CADDELL   *(laughs)* Sorry, in theatre, it's tradition to say that instead of saying *good luck*. It's actually seen as bad luck to say good luck, does that make sense?

LAINIE   Not really.

CADDELL   Fair enough. So . . . are you two ready?

LAINIE   *(grinning nervously)* I can't believe this is happening. My heart's beating a hundred miles an hour.

CADDELL   Mariam . . . you okay?

MARIAM   There's too many people out there.

LAINIE   I know. Have you seen the lobby? It's packed. Show's sold out.

CADDELL   Lainie . . .

LAINIE   *(realizing)* Sorry.

CADDELL   Mariam, you can do this. You know the lines. You know the fights. You're going to be fine. I know you don't believe me right now, but you might even have

63

a good time. Just think, those folks out there have no idea what they're about to see. They think you're just a couple of high school girls. They're not expecting our scene.

C'mon. Let's run through it one more time. The guys aren't ready yet, I'll play Romeo for this run. It'll calm your nerves.

Remember. Show speed. No faster. Clean. Sharp. Eye contact. Let's pick it up at the usual spot. I am for you?

They all get into position. LAINIE looks at MARIAM.

LAINIE   I am for you.

MARIAM nods. Gets into character.

MARIAM   *(as TYBALT) I am for you.*

They run the scene. Full speed. A showstopper of a fight. We hear a few key lines from the scene to help ground us in what is happening.

MERCUTIO   *Come, sir, your passado.*

ROMEO   *Hold Tybalt! Good Mercutio!*

MERCUTIO is stabbed. ROMEO helps him to a bench as TYBALT backs away.

MERCUTIO   *(to ROMEO) I am hurt. Is he gone and hath nothing?*

ROMEO   *I thought all for the best.*

MERCUTIO   *A plague on both your houses!*

MERCUTIO dies. ROMEO looks up at TYBALT.

ROMEO   *Mercutio's soul is but a little ways above our heads.*
Staying for thine to keep him company.

He attacks him. They fight.

TYBALT   *Thou wretched boy!*

ROMEO kills TYBALT. He realizes what he has done.

ROMEO   *O, I am fortune's fool!*

*The fight and the scene are over. Both MERCUTIO and TYBALT
lie dead on the stage.*

Shift.

*We are back in the present. CADDELL breaks the dramatic mo-
ment and smiles. He walks over and puts out his hand. He
pulls LAINIE up. Before CADDELL can help MARIAM up, LAINIE has
crossed to her. She puts her hand out.*

*A moment. Slowly, MARIAM takes her hand and LAINIE pulls
her up. CADDELL picks up one of the sabres off the floor.*

CADDELL   Okay. I can't believe I'm saying this, but go out there
and kick each other's butts.

*He doesn't say it but it's clear. He's proud of them. He tosses
LAINIE the sabre. He exits. LAINIE and MARIAM cross to opposite
sides of the stage. LAINIE stops.*

LAINIE   Hey. Break a leg.

She smiles. A small smile but a true one.

MARIAM   You too.

They exit.

END

ACKNOWLEDGEMENTS

This play grew out of a production of *Romeo and Juliet* that I performed in a few years ago at the University of Alberta for an MFA Directing student. Revisiting Lady Capulet (whom I played professionally in the mid 1990s) was a wonderful experience . . . although a few things did strike me as an older and perhaps more observant woman. Each night as we warmed up and prepared for the show, when the fight call was on and all the combat sequences run, it was interesting to note all the men in the play were onstage fighting and all the women were standing in the shadows watching. And it struck me . . . the great gender divide.

That same year, I had the pleasure of teaching acting at Artstrek, the fifty-plus-year-old residential drama camp for Alberta youth ages twelve to eighteen. The play we worked on, completely coincidentally, was again *Romeo and Juliet*. Seeing young people's incredible engagement with the characters, the themes, and the lessons of that play resonated for me, and I began to wonder about a play that might bring some of these ideas and observations together. Watching the stage combat master class that two of my colleagues taught to a group of rapt teens was the final nail in the coffin. I had my story. I had my age group. I had my title.

This play would not be here without the support of many artists and organizations. First, thanks to Concrete Theatre for supporting this script from the very beginning; to Alberta Theatre Projects and the Enbridge playRites Award for an Established Canadian Playwright, which generously financed my first draft; to Brian Quirt and the Banff Playwrights Colony who gave me a beautiful space to work on that first draft and wonderful actors to read (Sheldon Elter, Kris Joseph, Richard Lee, Monice Peter, and Pamela Mala Sinha); to Len Falkenstein and the NotaBle Acts Theatre Festival in Fredericton, who gave me a workshop and a fantastic public reading (Stephanie Doucette, Kelsey Hines, and Caleb Marshall); and finally to my dear friend and fight consultant J.P. Fournier, who has cheered me on and helped me so much with the stage combat content. As *my* former fight teacher, I know very well his ability to ignite a flame in his students about stage combat. Something I hope to pass on. Many thanks to his acting students at both Mount Royal University and the University of Alberta for their generous help and support as I developed the script.

Finally, a huge thank you to Caroline and Mary-Ellen for all your hard work and support, and to the brilliant cast: Patti, Sam, and Jon; the fantastic crew: Rachel and Josiah; and wonderful designers: Dave and Patrick for the care you brought to the show.

For all the girls who have ever stood on the sidelines watching a fight call. This is for you.

Mieko is a playwright, actor, and director working in theatre, film, and television. Her plays, which include *The Red Priest (Eight Ways To Say Goodbye)*, *The Blue Light*, *The Dada Play*, and *Nisei Blue*, have been nominated for several awards, including the Governor General's Literary Award for Drama and the City of Edmonton Book Prize. Mieko has also been the recipient of both the Carol Bolt Award and the Enbridge play-Rites Award for an Established Canadian Playwright. Her plays have been produced across Canada and the US and are translated into French, Russian, Czech, and Japanese. Mieko is co-founder and current Artistic Director of Concrete The-atre, a nationally recognized twenty-six-year-old TYA tour-ing company. She is currently working on four new projects: *Makepeace*, *Burning Mom*, *Consent*, and *Mariam* with Amena Shehab. She lives and works in Edmonton.

First edition: October 2016

Printed and bound in Canada by Imprimerie Gauvin, Gatineau

Cover illustration and design by Byron Eggenschwiler

PLAYWRIGHTS CANADA PRESS

202-269 Richmond St. W.
Toronto, ON
M5V 1X1

416.703.0013
info@playwrightscanada.com
playwrightscanada.com

A **bundled** eBook edition is available
with the purchase of this print book.

CLEARLY PRINT YOUR NAME ABOVE IN UPPER CASE

Instructions to claim your eBook edition:
1. Download the BitLit app for Android or iOS
2. Write your name in **UPPER CASE** above
3. Use the BitLit app to submit a photo
4. Download your eBook to any device

MIX
Paper from
responsible sources
FSC® C100212